Shetland Sheepdogs as Pets

The Handy Guide for Shetland Sheepdogs

Shetland Sheepdog General Info, Purchasing, Care, Keeping, Health, Supplies, Food, and More Included!

By: Lolly Brown

Copyrights and Trademarks

All rights reserved. No part of this book may be reproduced or transformed in any form or by any means, graphic, electronic, or mechanical, including photocopying, recording, taping, or by any information storage retrieval system, without the written permission of the author.

This publication is Copyright ©2020 NRB Publishing, an imprint. Nevada. All products, graphics, publications, software and services mentioned and recommended in this publication are protected by trademarks. In such instance, all trademarks & copyright belong to the respective owners. For information consult www.NRBpublishing.com

Disclaimer and Legal Notice

This product is not legal, medical, or accounting advice and should not be interpreted in that manner. You need to do your own due-diligence to determine if the content of this product is right for you. While every attempt has been made to verify the information shared in this publication, neither the author, neither publisher, nor the affiliates assume any responsibility for errors, omissions or contrary interpretation of the subject matter herein. Any perceived slights to any specific person(s) or organization(s) are purely unintentional.

We have no control over the nature, content and availability of the web sites listed in this book. The inclusion of any web site links does not necessarily imply a recommendation or endorse the views expressed within them. We take no responsibility for, and will not be liable for, the websites being temporarily unavailable or being removed from the internet.

The accuracy and completeness of information provided herein and opinions stated herein are not guaranteed or warranted to produce any particular results, and the advice and strategies, contained herein may not be suitable for every individual. Neither the author nor the publisher shall be liable for any loss incurred as a consequence of the use and application, directly or indirectly, of any information presented in this work. This publication is designed to provide information in regard to the subject matter covered.

Neither the author nor the publisher assume any responsibility for any errors or omissions, nor do they represent or warrant that the ideas, information, actions, plans, suggestions contained in this book is in all cases accurate. It is the reader's responsibility to find advice before putting anything written in this book into practice. The information in this book is not intended to serve as legal, medical, or accounting advice.

Foreword

The Shetland Sheepdog is also known as the Sheltie. They are one of the best companion dogs and also the smartest. They used to be a working dog and had performed very important jobs back in the day. They are used to experiencing labor especially in the rural areas of Scotland before they became a household dog that we now know of today. They are fun yet sensitive and just like many dog breeds, they crave for attention.

The Sheltie breed got their name because they hail from the Scottish island of Shetland. And until the first few years of the 20th century, the place was isolated but has since burst in other market. These dogs became herders and the natives of Shetland island don't want to feed them as much food compared to their larger dog cousins. Shetland sheepdog are tiny dogs but they have a lot of hair that serve as their protective layer that keeps them protected during summer and winter seasons.

In this book, you'll learn everything you need to know about Shetland Sheepdog from basic care to nutrition to important dog essentials. Are you ready to keep Shelties as pets? Let's get started!

Table of Contents

Shetland Sheepdog: The Farmer's Companion 1
    Is Sheltie the Right Breed for You? 2
    Shetland Sheepdog Breed History 4
    Arrival of the Sheltie 8

Chapter One: Identifying a Sheltie 11
    General Appearance 12
        Size, Proportion, Substance 12
        Life Expectancy 16
        The Athletic Sheltie 17
        Factors to Consider When Choosing a Sheltie 17
        What You Can Expect from a Sheltie Pup 20
        What You Can Expect from a Sheltered Sheltie 23

Chapter Two: The Sheltie Temperament and Traits 27
    Sheltie Traits 28
        Expression 28
        Intelligence and Training 28
        Shelties are Less Aggressive 29
        Shelties Are Born to be Cautious of Strangers 30
        Shelties with other Dogs 31
        Sheltie Natural Instincts 31

Shelties are Mostly Outdoor Dogs.................................... 32

Sheltie as a Family Dog 33

Shelties Have a Striking Appearance 33

Chapter Three: Costs of Keeping a Sheltie 35

How Much Does a Sheltie Cost?..................................... 36

Sheltie Adoption.. 37

Feeding Costs... 37

High Quality Food 38

Vet Expenses 39

Possible Vet Bills 39

Other Dog Keeping Costs 40

Chapter Four: Sheltie Starter Kit 41

Fun Loving Sheltie 42

Sheltie Starter Kit 43

Starter Kit #1 43

Starter Kit #2 45

Starter Kit #3 50

Starter Kit #4 51

Starter Kit #5 52

Starter Kit #6 52

Starter Kit #7 56

Chapter Five: Making Your Sheltie Feel At Home 59

Make Your Sheltie Feel Safe 60

House Rules for Shelties 61

Avoiding Poopy Accidents... 61

Fear of New Environment 62

Anxiety to a New Home 63

Prone to Aggression 64

Unwanted Behaviors 65

That Feeling of Danger 66

Rescue Dog's Past Experience 67

Issues with Multiple Pets or Shelties.. 67

Dominance Showdown 68

Getting Your Sheltie Familiar.. 69

Hyper Pups 70

Nippy Shelties 70

Chapter Six: Pet Insurance for Your Sheltie 73

Lifelong Pet Insurance... 75

Keeping Your Dog Safe 78

Keeping Your Pet Disciplined 79

Activities that Can Cause Injuries and What to Do 81

So You Don't Want a Pet Insurance? 82

Chapter Seven: Virus and Vaccines... 85

Parainfluenza Virus 87

Antibiotics 89

Antihistamine + Prednisolene 92

Vaccine 94

First Aid Kit 95

Handy First Aid Kit 95

First Aid Medications for Your Dog 97

Glossary of Dog Terms 101

Photo Credits 107

References 109

Shetland Sheepdog: The Farmer's Companion

If you ever visited a farm, you might find an adorable Shetland Sheepdog or two. Don't underestimate them because of their size. The dog's innate skill is to guard a farmer's garden from other animals and herd livestock, making this multi-tasking canine a good companion for farmers.

Intelligent to a fault, active, and eager to please, Shelties take well to training. Even though they're quite friendly with just about everybody, they are also very vigilant of their families. They're sensitive and shouldn't spend too many hours alone at home. Always keep a Sheltie mentally and physically stimulated with tasks, training, and exercise to make them a healthy and happy companion. Training them also prevents them from becoming troublesome dogs, so they are only for attentive dog lovers.

Nowadays, there are a lot of Shetland Sheepdog Mix Breeds as much as there are Shetland Sheepdog purebreds. And you may find them in shelters and rescues who are still waiting for responsible, loving homes to take them in.

Is Sheltie the Right Breed for You?

For you to know if a sheltie dog breed is right for you and your family, you need to take some time to properly socialize your pet so that they can get along well with other potential pets and people in general. Shetland Sheepdog are more suited for older kids than young ones because Shetland Sheepdog can easily get startled as they are quite sensitive to screams and loud noises.

And since Shetland Sheepdog have a tendency to keep things in order, your pet may tend to nip or growl at your child if he cannot be controlled. If your children learn to work with your pet, they can surely have a great time playing with one another and this can be a great exercising opportunity both for your dog and your kid. You'll find that Shetland Sheepdog are quite protective once they form a bond with you or your family. They tend to bark against people they don't know or if a stranger is approaching you.

Shetland Sheepdog gets along with other household pets like cats or dogs provided of course that they are properly introduced and socialized. Since Shetland Sheepdog are a relatively large – sized breed, they will tend to have a better relationship with larger breed dogs compared to smaller toy breeds as they could have dominant tendencies.

It's best to keep two Shetland Sheepdog, preferably a male and female, that's both neutered and around a year apart. If they are not neutered/ spayed then they will most likely have territoriality issues. Make sure to supervise your pet dog with another pet, be it a dog or cat, until you are sure that they're safe to be left with one another or until their relationship is already established. Keep in mind that Shetland Sheepdog are natural herders which could be a source of conflict with other animals.

Shetland Sheepdog Breed History

The ancestry of the Shetland Sheepdog date back to the rocky Shetland Islands of Scotland, which lie between Scotland and Norway, about 50 miles north of Scotland and a bit south of the Arctic Circle. These furry, short dogs came to be after farmers crossbred small all-purpose farm dogs of Scandinavian herding dog and Scottish Working Collie, owned by the crofters on the Shetland Islands. Later, there were some crosses with show Collies when the residents decided to breed them for show purposes.

The Sheltie dog is quite a newcomer in the world of purebred dogs. These dogs were first registered in 1908 in Lerwick which is near the area of Shetland Islands. The Shelties were eventually registered under the Scottish Shetland Sheepdog around 1909. Eventually both these kennel registries were recognized by the United Kingdom Kennel Club the same year.

The Sheltie were first registered as a Shetland Collie but because Collie dog breeders had some objections, the name was changed to Shetland Sheepdog around October of the same year. There was an article by a visitor to the islands describing the dogs as early as 1844. Other names include:

- Lilliputian Collie
- Toonie Dog
- Peerie Dog Fairy Dog
- Miniature Collie

On the islands, sheep typically were left to run virtually wild in the open country for most of the year and the area around. The small farms in Scotland, called crofts, were fenced to keep the farm animals out. Thus, the work of the early Shelties included keeping livestock away from the crofts. And because of their dog ancestors, they are proven to be excellent in rounding up animals - sheep, cattle, ponies, poultry - and serving as watchdogs and family companions.

Shetland Sheepdog: The Farmer's Companion

Shelties have continued to be used as working stock dogs, especially in mainland Britain and in the United States than on the Shetland Islands, ironically.

The beginnings of the Shetland Sheepdog breed was influenced by a Spitz breed that's brought from the Scandinavia region including the Pomeranian breed, Scotch Collie and a King Charles Spaniel. The original mix of the Sheltie breed is still quite unknown and debated to this day.

The Shetland Sheepdogs also became a source of income for the Shetland islanders after some tourists saw the breed and wanted to have a dog companion that's small and fluffy. Despite the color, size and type difference, any dog breed is acceptable in the island. One of those who got interested was James Loggie. He is a dog breeder who also promoted the Shetland Sheepdog and pioneered breeding smaller versions of Collie breed dogs that later became Shelties. Some of the crossbreeds were recorded but a lot were not.

There are suspicions and rumors of crosses with other breeds. Unknown for certain is where the blue, either bi-blue, or blue merle with tan had its beginnings. Today there can still be size differences in any given litter, tracing back to the smaller dogs or to the larger Collie. In the UK at the time, these crosses were acceptable provided the progeny was bred back for three generations to a Shetland Sheepdog. After the required three generations, the get would be registered as purebred Shelties. Mary Van Wagenen, the first breed historian in the USA, and she established the American version of Sheltland Sheepdog. Catherine Coleman Moore made a trip to England, and with Miss Clara Bowring, approached the English Kennel club to have those notations removed.

The trip was fruitful and subsequent imports were thereafter accepted by the AKC. Catherine was a founding member of the American Shetland Sheepdog Club, in February 1929. She was an early importer of the breed, the ASSA's first secretary and registered the first litter of Shelties recorded with the AKC. The English Shetland Sheepdog Club (ESSC) had been founded in 1914. Miss Bowring was the ESSC's secretary, an early Sheltie breeder and a wealthy patron of the breed.

The Sheltie also appears in the Herding Group and Pastoral Group in American and England respectively. The original purpose of the Sheltie dog was to become an all-around type of farm dog. The Sheltie breed assisted in doing livestock and anything that the crofters might need. These dogs are great family companion, and they even warning of potential house intruders. The tendency to bark is sometimes considered a liability in the Sheltie breed today. Whatever their task or responsibility, it was necessary for these early Shelties to earn their keep.

Arrival of the Sheltie

In 1908, Shelties came to the USA but unfortunately they didn't carry on. The AKC or American Kennel Club only recognized the Sheltie breed around 1911. And due to the Collie crossbreed listed in imported dog pedigrees, many of the early import Shelties weren't eligible for AKC registration because it was deemed as impure breeding. One such imported dog was already a breed Champion in the UK. At one time there were only two registered males in the USA eligible for breeding.

Shetland Sheepdog: The Farmer's Companion

The world wars had sort of an influence on the breeds that was imported to the American and what was bred from in the England. The difference in the size and type can be seen in the American and British version of the dog. The major difference between the two breed versions is the size. The British standard has a size 14 ½ inches for males and 14 inches for females, and states that a difference of more than one inch either way is highly undesirable.

While the standard in the American version does not specify size differences according to sex, but has a disqualification for measuring either under 13 inches or over 16 inches at the shoulder. The only other disqualification is brindle coloring, and more than 50% white in the show ring will get penalized, and white body spots is listed as being undesirable.

In 1914, the first American Sheltie breed champion was crowned followed by the first champion of the British version. Today, Shetland Sheepdog are excelling in different venues all over the world. Some Sheltie finds their place as therapy dogs and medical alert dogs while others are used in different fields. This dog excels in herding, obedience, agility and other dog events. But best of all, they are well – loved as a family pet.

Initially, Shetland Sheepdog was called the Shetland Collie. But this caused disagreements among the Rough Collie breeders of the time. For many years, Shelties had the name *Toonie* as the word means "farm" in Norwegian. Due to their stout build, they are called Dwarf Scotch Shepherd, Miniature Collie, and Lilliputian Collie. They are now widely nicknamed Shelties, and that's the name that we will use mostly on this guide book.

Chapter One: Identifying a Sheltie

The Shetland Sheepdog has many similarities with the Rough Collie because they have the same ancestors, the Working Collies of Scotland, and a variety of miniature long-haired Scottish dog breeds. Although the parallels between the Shetland Sheepdog and the Rough Collie is marked, there are still some differences. The Shetland Sheepdog is a small, active, rough-coated, long-haired working dog. It must be sound, athletic, and muscular. The outline should be so balanced that no part appears out of proportion to the whole. Studs should appear masculine; bitches feminine.

Chapter One: Identifying a Sheltie

General Appearance

Size, Proportion, Substance

The Shetland Sheepdog stands between 13 and 16 inches at the shoulder. Its body should appear fairly long as measured from shoulder joint to ischium.

Coat

A Shetland Sheepdog has a hairy double coat that is long and is abundant all over the body but is shorter on the head and legs. The outercoat is straight and rough, while the undercoat is fluffy yet tight. The hair on the face, tips of ears, and feet should be silky. Mane and frill should is abundant and particularly impressive in males. The hair on tail profuse. The downside, like all very furry dogs, their thick coats will result in a lot of shedding.

Color

Shelties are a sight to behold. They are one of those breeds that are beautiful to look at because each comes in a dual or variety of colors that flow well with their long fluffy fur. These dogs generally come in three broad strokes: Sable, Black, and Blue Merle. And with differing amounts of tan, mahogany, black, gray, and white fur, the dogs have official fur colors such as Sable, Tri-Color, Bi Black, Blue Merle, and Bi Blue.

Head

When viewed from top or side, the Sheltie's head is long, blunt wedge tapering slightly from ears to nose.

Eyes

Sheltie's lovable eyes are medium size with dark, almond-shaped rims, set somewhat obliquely in the skull. Most Shelties have dark-colored eyes except for Blue Merles, who have astonishingly blue or merle optics.

Ears

Their eyes are small and flexible, placed high, carried three-fourths erect, with tips breaking forward. When the dog is calm, the ears fold lengthwise and thrown back into the frill.

Skull and Muzzle

Underneath a Sheltie's cute long face is a flat skull that is of equal length of the muzzle, which its balance point is the inner corner of the eye. Its cheeks are flat and merge smoothly into a well-rounded muzzle. The dog's jaws should be kept clean and are powerful. Their deep under jaw, which is rounded at the chin, should extend to the base of the nostril. Its nose is black, and lips are tight that must meet and fit smoothly together all the way around. Teeth level and evenly placed.

Neck, Topline, Body

A healthy Sheltie has a sinewy neck, arched, and of sufficient length to carry the head. The back should be level and sturdy. Its chest should be deep and its brisket reaching to the point of the elbow. Its ribs should be well sprung but flattened at their lower half to allow movement of the foreleg and shoulder. The dog's abdomen is moderately tucked up. There should be a slight arch at the loins, and the croup should slope continuously to the rear. The pelvic should be set at a 30-degree angle to the vertebrae

Tail

The Sheltie's tail is long and lies along the back edge of the hind legs that the last part of the spine will reach the hock joint. The carriage of the tail at rest is straight down or in a slight upward curve. When the dog is alert, it will lift its tail but will not curve it forward over the back.

Chapter One: Identifying a Sheltie

Forequarters

The Sheltie's shoulder blades should slope at a 45-degree angle forward and downward to the shoulder joints. At the withers, they are separated only by the vertebra, but they must angle outward adequately to hold the desired spring of rib. The upper arm joins the shoulder blade at as nearly as possible a right angle. The dog's elbow joint is equidistant from the ground and the withers. Healthy Shelties have forelegs that are straight and muscular. Their patterns are very strong, sinewy, and flexible. Feet should be elliptical and tight with the toes well arched and fittingly close together. The pup's pads are deep and tough, their nails hard and strong.

Hindquarters

The Sheltie's thighs are broad and muscular. Stifle bones join the thigh bone and are precisely angled at the stifle joint. The general length of the stifle should at least equal to the length of the thigh bone and preferably slightly exceed it. The Hock joint should be definite, angular, brawny, with good bone and strong ligamentation. The hock (metatarsus) should be small and straight viewed from all angles.

Chapter One: Identifying a Sheltie

Gait

The ambling gait of the Shetland Sheepdog bespeaks uncomplicated quickness and elegance. Healthy and happy dogs walk with no jerkiness, nor stiff, stilted, up-and-down movement.

Temperament

Like many other herding breeds, the Sheltie likes to show-off its natural herding instincts, particularly on animals and children. Depending on the upbringing, an emotionally and mentally healthy Shetland Sheepdog is intensely loyal, affectionate, and responsive to his owner. It is cautious toward strangers but not to the point of showing fear or cringing. Such as there are happy Shelties, it is not impossible to find one that is either shy, timid, nervousness, stubborn, snappy, or has an ill temper. Lots of training and tender loving care will help rehabilitate an unhappy Sheltie.

Life Expectancy

Lucky are Sheltie owners for their furry companions can live up to approximately 14 to 16 years as long as they

Chapter One: Identifying a Sheltie

take care of them. Dog parents should take their fur kids to regular yearly check-ups with a veterinarian to screen for any potential health problems.

The Athletic Sheltie

If you want your Sheltie to enter dog competitions such as herding competitions, athletic events, fly – dog, and obedience competitions, you can expect them to excel at these kinds of events provided of course that you help them when it comes to training and other athletic/ intelligence demands that these competitions require.

Shetland Sheepdog could get intimidated by large crowds and other animals around which is why it's best to socialize them so that they are comfortable when joining events. If you are considering your pet to compete, it's probably best to hire a professional dog trainer so that your dog can maximize its potential. Competitions will be a rewarding experience for both you and y our dog, such events can also form a strong and bonded relationship.

Factors to Consider When Choosing a Sheltie

For male Shelties they are generally larger which means that they would eat more – which also means that

Chapter One: Identifying a Sheltie

you need to buy more food compared to female Shetland Sheepdog. They are also are much stronger, bulkier, and taller than females. This could be a concern if you have smaller – size pets around like poodles or small cat breeds. A male Shetland Sheepdog will eat more food compared to non – pregnant female Shetland Sheepdog. Oftentimes they are usually more aggressive and also independent. Shetland Sheepdog may be quite difficult to manage if you only live in a small and confined house because they won't have outlet for their energy.

Generally have territoriality issues especially if there's another male species around. This is also true if there are female dogs around that are in their heat period. They usually establish a close relationship to their owner compared to females that can equally form a bond with people other than their main keeper. Shelties will require more exercise and playtime. They also tend to be more difficult to introduce to new pets and socialize compared to female Shetland Sheepdog.

Chapter One: Identifying a Sheltie

Male Shetland Sheepdog reach sexual maturity earlier than females. Their sexual tendencies can already be seen at a young age, and this could be a problem if you own other female dog breeds. Don't be surprised if your male Sheltie roams around the house or even in your neighborhood because this means that they probably have smelled a female dog that's in heat and they're pursuing it.

When it comes to choosing female dogs are smaller in size and are generally less aggressive. Most female dogs only become aggressive when they gave birth to their pups but this is because they're just protecting their litter. Female dogs are less active compared to male Shetland Sheepdog and they are also generally easier to train. They usually get shy and scared if anyone treated them in a harsh way or scold them in an angry voice. Females tend to get along with people other than their owners. And they are also easier to introduce and socialize with other household pets.

Shelties don't get along if they are housed with another female, and this may result to conflict which is why it's best to pair them up with a male if you want to keep two Shetland Sheepdog. Group of female Shetland Sheepdog will form a hierarchy, and will bond with each other once the pecking order is established.

What You Can Expect from a Sheltie Pup

Young Shetland Sheepdog will surely brighten you and your family's day the moment you wake up in the morning, and that's puppies are obviously the cutest and most adorable stage in any dog's life. If you want to soak in their lovable and energetic personalities then consider getting a pup instead of an adult.

Getting a puppy is best suited for individuals and families who can spend quality time with a young dog. If you plan on raising your Sheltie according to your standards, and you're focus on properly training them to meet you/ your family's want or needs, then you'll have better chances with a pup compared to an adult. You need to spend quality time with your Sheltie pup and form a bond with them so that they will be easier to train or socialize.

Chapter One: Identifying a Sheltie

Some people get a pup but they are not in the house all the time or they don't take the time to train them, and they wonder why their pets are misbehaving.

If you want your Sheltie to become a well – behaved pet as it grows, you must give time and attention to it, and not just provide their basic needs. Buying a puppy from a reputable source or rescue shelter will make the dog stay longer as part of your family since it'll recognize that you're the one providing them with all their basic needs and general care as they grow. They'll recognize that they're part of the pack.

Prior to buying a puppy from the breeder, it's best that you take the time to see how they interact and play with other dogs as this will give you a hint when it comes to temperament/ personality. Usually, puppies who grew in a litter tend to be more assertive and aggressive than puppies who are raised alone which is why the former might be harder to train. The latter though may tend to be more reserved especially with strangers, which is why socialization at an early age is important.

Chapter One: Identifying a Sheltie

Some owners find it difficult to manage and raise a pup especially if they have their own families to take care of. You have to keep in mind that raising a puppy whether it's a Sheltie breed or not is very similar to having a baby. You are responsible 24/7 especially in the first few months. You need to ensure that you have the time to let your pup meet new people, other pets, and take them out for a walk around the neighborhood.

As puppies grow, you'll soon find out that they can be just like a child. If you're sort of a neat freak and you want everything organize around the house, getting a puppy may not be best for you because at some point they can damage your furniture and other household items especially when they undergo the "chewing stage." You need to puppy – proof your house and also housebreak your pup. If you want training to be effective, you have to be consistent with your methods and the schedule otherwise it could be difficult for you and your pup. You have to have lots of patience if you plan on getting a pup.

Chapter One: Identifying a Sheltie

What You Can Expect from a Sheltered Sheltie

Some keepers find it more advantageous to acquire an adult Sheltie because you easily know its overall appearance and size as well as its personality and behavior. Most adult dogs are socialized, trained and housebroken already which means that it can save you time and skip all the difficult parts of dog keeping – not to mention your patience and furniture!

If you acquire your adult Sheltie from a reputable breeder, the dog will most likely be trained already. You can expect him/her to already know how to behave around the house, on the leash, or whenever you're out for a walk. Training is still a must but it'll be less time consuming since they're already matured compared to training a pup. Same amount of love and care is needed but less emphasis on training concepts.

Most matured Shetland Sheepdog tend to be calmer when introduced to a new surrounding which is why you won't have a problem once you bring your pet home

Chapter One: Identifying a Sheltie

although introduction, socialization, and housebreaking must still be taught. An adult Sheltie may take just a few days to adjust to its new environment so just give them time to settle and bond with them often so that they will get to establish a relationship with you and your family.

The biggest disadvantage of buying an adult dog is that it'll be harder to change any of the negative behavior they may have. If you find that your dog adapted a bad habit from its previous owner, it might be very difficult to correct. It's still possible to re – train your dog but it could be confusing for your pet. You will need to take effort if you want to change a particular habit you don't like and encourage them with treats or use positive reinforcement. Patience is a must if this is going to be your problem.

If you find that your adult Sheltie doesn't listen to you or are showing signs of misbehaving, make sure to take the time to give them positive attention and socialize with them so that they'll develop a good relationship with you. Some adults may find it hard to settle in a new environment and this is where they usually become difficult to handle.

Chapter One: Identifying a Sheltie

Adult Shetland Sheepdog may also be harder to introduce and/ or socialize with your other household pets, which is why you need to ensure that you monitor them whenever they're interacting with one another. If you have a smaller breed of dogs or cats, it might be more difficult since Shetland Sheepdog tend to herd things and show dominance to smaller animals.

When it comes to basic needs, it's almost the same with puppies. Make sure that your adult dog is getting the right amount of food, has enough space around the house where they can have exercising opportunities, and that their health is taken care of. You will need to make sure that they're neutered/ spayed them.

Chapter One: Identifying a Sheltie

Chapter Two: The Sheltie Temperament and Traits

Now that you've learn the origin and biological information of the Shetland Sheepdog, it's time to learn the temperament and traits of the Sheltie to know if this is truly the dog you and/ or your family can get along with.

The Shetland Sheepdog is a very smart, and active dog that's very easy to train. They are deemed as world – class when it comes to competitions especially in obedience, herding and agility. They are very intuitive and loyal making them great therapy dogs.

Chapter Two: The Sheltie Temperament and Traits

Their affectionate and affable nature makes them great family pets but they can also be excellent watchdog. While the Sheltie still excels at herding, today this vocal breed is more often seen as a farm dog and family pet or companion dog, thanks to both its beauty and kindness. The Sheltie is very fluffy small breeds that are a leader in its own world. In this chapter you'll learn why Shetland Sheepdog is one of the best family dogs you'll ever have.

Sheltie Traits

Expression

We can see the expression of the Sheltie by the combinations of its head, the shape, use, and set of its ears and eyes. Its usual facial expression should be alert, gentle, intelligent, and questioning. Toward strangers, the eyes should show awareness and calmness, but no fear.

Intelligence and Training

Like any other herding and working breed, Shetland Sheepdogs are very intelligent and are known for their

Chapter Two: The Sheltie Temperament and Traits

success in obedience training. Foundations of this statement include many findings that suggest herding breeds, like the Sheltie, are one of the easiest breed types to train. Examples of the findings include a 2005 study by researchers Serpell and Hsu. They conclude the study to be so. However, some studies suggest the Shetland Sheepdogs fall in the middle when it comes to trainability for certain tasks.

Because they are super smart, fur parents of Shelties need to schedule training and playing time with them because they need the stimulation to keep them happy. If not, they might find other troublesome ways to use all of their brain energy, such as ruining furniture or harming other creatures, including humans.

Shelties are Less Aggressive

A study suggests that Shetland Sheepdogs have a low reactivity rate to new stimuli, such as a doorbell ringing, sounds of airplane zooming in the sky, or other loud sudden noises. The finding suggests Shelties are good at staying calm in surprising situations.

However, another research showed that Shetland Sheepdogs scored higher than average on stranger-directed aggression. But they also garnered a lower than average grade on owner-directed aggression! The study supports the strong bonds that Shetland Sheepdogs are known to make to their close human companions. It also suggests that Shetland Sheepdogs are more prone to fear than actual aggression, which leads us to…

Shelties Are Born to be Cautious of Strangers

There is a survey that suggests that Shelties score higher than average on stranger-directed fear, which makes early socialization important when it comes to helping reduce this potential aggression towards unfamiliar people. Introducing your Sheltie puppy to as many new environments as possible while young will help them be happier and more outgoing around strangers as adults. Fear can result in unwanted aggression. And although we don't want our dogs to show hostility, we also don't want them to be scared or unhappy!

Chapter Two: The Sheltie Temperament and Traits

Shelties with other Dogs

If you want a new dog in your family but already own other canines, you'll need a breed that likes their future siblings. Shelties score much lower than average on dog-directed aggression. They have the lowest mean score of the 11 breeds in this study! Shetland Sheepdogs tend to be a peaceful breed that gets along well with other dogs. However, if your other dogs are small you need to be aware of the Sheltie's instincts. Speaking of instincts....

Sheltie Natural Instincts

Some Sheltie instincts can be tough to control, even with training. The Shetland Sheepdog temperament is affected by some strong instincts.

Shelties are known for trying to chase things in motion, such as passing vehicles, bicycles, and even small running animals or children. Although Shetland Sheepdogs don't mean any injury with these behaviors, they can occasionally even nip at heels when herding. Plus, if your Sheltie tries to chase vehicles, it can be dangerous for your

Chapter Two: The Sheltie Temperament and Traits

pup! You can try to control these instincts by keeping your Sheltie on a leash and harness when walking outside.

Also, Shelties are known for being vocal dogs. Herding breeds often use barking to assist in their job. So, don't be shocked if you get a Sheltie that barks quite a lot! These instincts can be complicated to control in the home. If you have small children or other small pets that run around your abode a lot, consider these instincts before getting a Shetland Sheepdog and train them or have them enroll in a school for dogs, and if you can tolerate frequent barking.

Shelties are Mostly Outdoor Dogs

Herding breeds like the Sheltie enjoy lively playing and exercise more than other breed types. Your Shetland Sheepdog will appreciate nothing more than running around and having fun with you. So, if you're looking for a dog that enjoys showing its love by cuddling up on the sofa with you all day, this isn't the best choice.

Chapter Two: The Sheltie Temperament and Traits

Sheltie as a Family Dog

These spirited herding dogs make strong bonds with their families. So, they are excellent for those wanting a loyal dog. But, again, families with young children or other pets should be aware of instincts that can lead to chasing or nipping. Training a Sheltie to avoid nipping other pets and humans is possible but needs a lot of time and effort.

Some parents do find the herding skills of the Sheltie useful when it comes to rounding rowdy kids. However, these parents need to make sure the Sheltie does not bite or nip.

Shelties Have a Striking Appearance

Shelties are good – looking dogs and that's usually the first thing that people noticed. As mentioned earlier, the Sheltie that we have today emerged from a line of Scandinavian herding dogs around early 20th century. These dogs were also crossed with small dog breeds like Spaniels and Pomeranians.

Chapter Two: The Sheltie Temperament and Traits

The Shetland farmers bred these dogs to be fluffy and cute looking so they could sell them to the tourists who came by. They were a hit! It's because never before had anyone seen a mini working dog breed like a Sheltie.

Chapter Three: Costs of Keeping a Sheltie

The Sheltie is an affectionate and affable breed. It's one of the most popular dog breeds in the world. For many dog lovers, purchasing a Sheltie is worth it because it's a one – of – a kind breed. The price will vary depending on different factors such as the breeder that you'll get it from, how many pups you're willing to buy, the age, health conditions, pedigree, lineage etc. Not only that, you need to also factor in other costs for dog upkeep such as food, vet care, shelter and supplies etc.

Chapter Three: Costs of Keeping a Sheltie

How Much Does a Sheltie Cost?

As mentioned earlier, the price of the Sheltie varies greatly, more so than other dog breeds. On average, you can expect to pay around a thousand dollars, more or less. Take note though that if you're looking to buy a "cheap" Sheltie pup, you are most likely getting one from a backyard breeder without AKC documentation. Even if you bought it from a pet store, it doesn't mean that the breed you're buying is of great quality. Most pet stores get their animals from puppy mills and some even from illegal sources where animals are not treated properly.

On the other hand, Sheltie that came from excellent lineage or those with special traits usually cost more. It's obviously more expensive but keep in mind that it also means the pup you're getting is healthy and raised properly. This means that it will be less expensive in terms of vet bills in the long run. If you're looking to acquire a pup from a champion lineage, then expect to pay more.

Chapter Three: Costs of Keeping a Sheltie

Sheltie Adoption

One of the best ways to save money is through adopting a Sheltie. Pet adoption will just cost your around $500. It usually includes vaccinations and proper documentation. This is a much better alternative if you're on a budget but still want to get a relatively quality dog breed. You will also be saving a life at the same time. It's a win – win for everyone!

Feeding Costs

These dogs are relatively medium – size breeds and they are very active. It also equates to more food per month compared to other smaller dog breeds. They are the kinds of dogs that won't leave anything on their plate – they just love to eat. Given the affinity of the Sheltie food, you should have computed on how much their food will cost you and if you can afford it, before you even acquire one.

Chapter Three: Costs of Keeping a Sheltie

High Quality Food

Just like any dog breed, it's highly recommended that you provide them with high – quality food because this will make them strong as it grows. The amount that your pet will eat depends on their current size, activity level, age and gender. Sometimes it also depends on whether or not they have an existing condition. The amount of food can range around 2 1/2 cups to 4 1/2 cups per day for an adult. Make sure to ask your vet regarding the specific amount of food your dog needs.

On average, quality dog food will cost $2 to $3 per pound. Of course, you can't also forget the treats; you need to provide a treat for your pet especially if you will train them. All dogs need treats as a reward for having a good behavior. You should budget around $10 per month for this.

Chapter Three: Costs of Keeping a Sheltie

Vet Expenses

Generally speaking, the Sheltie is a healthy breed. But of course, as mentioned earlier, this is not guaranteed if you purchase one from backyard breeders or pet stores. If you buy a quality dog breed, then you won't have anything to worry. Still, there are some basic vet cares you need to do.

If your pet is not neutered/ spayed, then you should do this right away otherwise you will have unexpected offspring. However, if you have plans on breeding your pet then you won't have to pay for this. The surgery will cost around $300 to $500.

Possible Vet Bills

The most common and perhaps one of the most expensive health issues for dogs in general is cancer. This is according to the Sheltie Club of America. They may also be prone to heart diseases, hip and elbow dysplasia as well as eye diseases. The most common health issues of this breed and their approximate treatment costs might range from as low as $200 to as high as $5000. On average, you will only pay a couple of bucks for a healthy Sheltie just for regular

Chapter Three: Costs of Keeping a Sheltie

check – ups and maybe some occasional health issues like kennel cough etc.

Other Dog Keeping Costs

Aside from the initial purchase price and vet needs, there are also other things you need to keep in mind if you've decided to keep a dog in general. You may want to enroll your pet in an obedience training program which may cost you around $50 to $125 for a couple of weeks sessions. Fortunately, Shelties are one of the most intelligent and trainable breeds in the world.

Other things will include food, grooming, toys, crate, vitamins/ supplements, boarding etc. It will likely cost you around $1,600 on average per year to provide all of your Sheltie's needs.

Chapter Four: Sheltie Starter Kit

The Sheltie breed is known for being playful, cheerful and active. In fact, they are also one of the friendliest dogs that exist today. As a keeper of this dog breed, it's essential to keep your schedule free at least once or twice a week so that you can take your pet for a walk since they need exercise and they are the kinds of dogs that are not contented with being at home all day.

They aren't the best fit for an owner who's inactive or maybe a senior citizen already since they are not the lap – dog types. Despite their active energy; the Sheltie breed can still remain tolerant and calm which makes them perfect for a family with kids. For a Sheltie, having average energy usually means that they have high energy when compared to other dog breed; but it's necessary because this is where Sheltie relies upon for whatever task it is required to do. In fact, the energy level it possesses makes it quite nimble and requires a release of energy every day in order to keep its right weight since most Shelties are inclined to put on an extra weight especially when they are inactive.

Fun Loving Sheltie

Shelties are usually characterized in having a mild temperament which is why you may often see this dog breed playing around with kids and another pet making them an ideal family pet dog. When a Sheltie dog is hanging out with his keepers, it usually exhibits a trait of obedience, and they can also be quite endearing when they're shown care and love.

Shelties are renowned for being a breed with a vibrant and fun-loving nature. What's important for potential owners though is whether these dogs are child-friendly pets and how well suited they are to family life.

Chapter Four: Sheltie Starter Kit

When you're bringing a pet into your family home, it's important that you choose one that has a calm yet playful temperament. Just like children, part of the Sheltie's personality and traits love playing and are energetic happy pets. They have a great degree of warmth about them but can show a mischievous and disobedient side which is more endearing than irritating. However, one thing that's important to remember is that they need to be introduced to families at a young age so they can socialize accordingly. If you adopt an older Sheltie they could be troublesome and harder to train.

Sheltie Starter Kit

Starter Kit #1

Shelties love to play a lot and they can run around the yard without showing any signs of tiredness. These dogs require lots of activity which means you need to do regular walk in the park and various activities that can keep boredom at bay, and it can also help maintain their weight. But of course, like humans they also need some rest which is why picking the best dog crate is one of the first basic things you need to get for your Sheltie starter pack.

Factors to Consider When Choosing a Dog Crate

Obviously, you want something that's completely dog - safe, and built with rounded edges so your Sheltie won't get unneeded injuries from walking around the pet crate. You want something that's covered with a non - toxic coating so that even when your Sheltie chews on it, he/ she won't ingest any toxic. It's also important that the crate has slide - bolt latches for safeguarding your Sheltie but this is optional.

There are also puppy crates that come with a divider panel. This feature enables you to easily adjust the crate according to your Sheltie's dimension. Sheltie pups while they are small will certainly want a spacious and comfy crate. It's also good that the crate comes with removable plastic trays so that you can have the option of just gliding the tray from underneath, easily clean it up and put it back to place.

Chapter Four: Sheltie Starter Kit

There are also crates that come with optional double doors, though it might be a little more expensive than a single – door type of crate. It will probably be a better option if you can easily access the inside of your Sheltie's crate so you can place things like dog bowls, feeders, toys, sheets, or anything else.

The standard crate for a Sheltie may not necessarily require dual doors. The built - in handles will surely be helpful. Having a removable plastic tray is also perfect while housetraining your Sheltie. It's practically unavoidable they'll have mishaps in the dog crate.

Starter Kit #2

Shelties are dedicated, dynamic and their limitless energy definitely makes for an enjoyable time! Shelties are generally easy – going pets, they are quite easy to please, and like all dogs they are also people – pleasers! So that's a win – win! Shelties take pleasure in roaming around the house which is why you need to constantly keep them engage and interact with them through playtime and games. The next starter kit is all about fun with dog toys!

Chapter Four: Sheltie Starter Kit

A dog's seeker instincts provide them the tendency to gnaw on anything they can find. To stop this destructive behavior from worsening, it's wise to provide them playthings that they can actually chew whenever they want to. The toys must be strong enough to endure constant chewing as well as pulling, providing your Sheltie their much needed urge to chew something. There is various other types of toys that can satisfy and keep your Shelties occupied but make sure to include a chewy toy in the roster.

Teether toys are essential for Sheltie puppies. You need to provide the appropriate toys during the teething stage; otherwise you can expect your puppy Sheltie would most definitely eat anything from clothes and accessories to your most precious furniture. Sorry to say but with your Sheltie or with any other dog for that matter, nothing is safe! Providing them with puppy teether toys is not just beneficial for them but also safe for your house because they can also chew through electrical cables if you don't give them a proper outlet.

Considering that your Sheltie puppy will certainly be irritated as their teeth grow which is why it's best to offer

Chapter Four: Sheltie Starter Kit

them perhaps various forms or types of chew toys. We recommend that you provide a few chew toy samplings and then let your Sheltie pup decide what he/she wants so as to eliminate the discomfort or pain in this teething stage.

Selecting Sheltie Toys

Shelties are the social type. When you leave them alone in the house, it's ideal to provide them a space where they can be free to let go of that extra energy. A buddy toy might be best for your pet. A companion toy will certainly keep them entertained especially if they don't have other dogs to play with. It's also best to pick a soft resilient toy that is large enough for your Sheltie to enjoy.

When it comes to selecting toys, you would want to choose something that can sort of mimic body warmth, giving your Sheltie much more complacency. Make sure that the toy is durable and easy to clean.

You might need to also provide toys that can make your pet have fun and also keep them active at the same

Chapter Four: Sheltie Starter Kit

time because they require physical activity to keep them healthy. This is why choosing interactive activities can be hitting two birds with one stones.

Other than strolling your Sheltie daily, choose playthings that you can enjoy along with them! Playing a game of fetch is an excellent place to start, and you would certainly want the best toy for this. This is why lots of keepers go – to choice are Frisbees. If you live in an area where there are lots of space that your Sheltie can roam around in like a park or beach, it will be a good bonding task for you and your pet to walk there and also play catch. It will surely let your Sheltie to run around and have that natural exercise for them while they're having fun.

The More Options the Better

Having a handful of toy samples initially will certainly help so you can identify what type of toy your Sheltie might like, but keep in mind that you don't need to stock up on lots of toys as this might also make your dog feel overwhelmed. Make sure the playthings you pick are not just enjoyable for you Sheltie but can also be good for their

Chapter Four: Sheltie Starter Kit

physical health and mental stimulation. It's also important to keep in mind that as your Sheltie develops, their needs change also! Some older Shelties won't have the ability to chew on certain types of chew toys and some games will not be applicable anymore once they outgrow them. When your Sheltie reaches their golden years, soft toys are the most appropriate choice.

Make sure to clean your pet's toys because it will certainly have all sorts of dirt in it over time like saliva, dust, and other things, which can turn them into smelly toys. Use soap and warm water to clean them, and make sure to completely dry them thoroughly prior to letting your Sheltie play again with it. Keep your Sheltie healthy and happy with the best toys but nothing beats your bonding with them.

Chapter Four: Sheltie Starter Kit

Starter Kit #3

Leashes are beneficial for numerous factors. One of which is that it disperse the pressure points from your dog's body when you walk him compared to having a chain around its neck. An appropriate dog harness will prevent your Sheltie from getting injured.

There are different styles of dog leash, so if you want to identify the best one for your Sheltie, you need to know what kind of leash to look for. The most important parts are the bands, the rings or sliders, and the vest. The equipment is typically plastic or metal, the bands are typically made from polyester or nylon, and also the vests are usually made from a nylon, or polyester, with a breathable mesh cellular lining.

The dog harnesses that are available today sometimes include extra padding or vests. There are also some that have ornaments while others are no – pull types of leash. A no – pull leash are great choices for some Shelties who are not fond of pulling or going all over while walking. When it comes to choosing a type of dog harness, just make sure that

Chapter Four: Sheltie Starter Kit

the type of leash you choose will suit your Sheltie in any kind of activity.

When it comes to sizes, dog harness comes in various lengths, and each of those dimensions can be readjusted. This is due to the fact that the different sizing combinations will make the keeper discover what best fits for their dog. Sizing is necessary when it pertains to harnesses. If it is too tight, then it could cause injury. If it's too loose, your Sheltie might be able to escape.

Starter Kit #4

Another important thing to always have a lot of is dog food. Make sure to have this ready once your pup arrives. You need to ask your breeder as to what kind of diet your pup has and try to continue that by buying the same brand or offering the same amount. If you want to change their diet, make sure to do it in a gradual way so as not to upset your pup's stomach. What you can do is to combine the old diet with the new so that transition is gradual. Let your pup adjust to the new diet to prevent diarrhea. Since pups are quite active animals, you need to make sure that

Chapter Four: Sheltie Starter Kit

you buy a food/ water bowl that can't be easily tipped over. You need to replenish clean water 2 times a day. Some keepers use automatic feeders but it's just optional.

Starter Kit #5

The next starter kit you'll need are grooming materials. The things you'll need for grooming will depend if your pet's coat is longhaired or shorthaired. Make sure to ask the breeder regarding what age you can start trimming your pup's coat. Usually, you need to wait until the puppy is already 10 months old. Ask your vet or breeder about it.

Starter Kit #6

When giving nutrition for your Sheltie, just make sure that you never feed your pet more than the amount he/ she needs. Consult your breeder and you're your veterinarian for advice on whether your Sheltie needs more food or maybe additional supplements and vitamins. Don't make the mistake of feeding your Sheltie more or less food just because of his/ her appearance. Some keepers think that dog

Chapter Four: Sheltie Starter Kit

breeds are omnivores because they eat both veggies and meat which is a fact but that's only because they would pretty much eat anything. Keep in mind that Sheltie are carnivores by nature. Their digestive system is naturally set to digest meat since they have strong and powerful digestive juices. Dogs in general are designed to eat flesh meat. If you study their anatomy, dogs have short intestines and they also have strong jaw bones, and sharp teeth that are meant to cut and rip meats. Although they can eat other type of foods like vegetables or human scrapes, their primary diet should be carnivorous.

Most keepers switch foods once their puppies hit 9 months. We highly recommend that you first consult your breeder or vet before changing your Sheltie's diet so that you can be sure as to what age is appropriate for the diet switch. Some people introduce adult food earlier than nine months, while some do it a little over ten months which is why it's best to ask your vet or breeder since they already have knowledge and experience regarding this matter.

Chapter Four: Sheltie Starter Kit

One of the first things that you need to consider when it comes to feeding your Sheltie is whether you should feed dry or wet food, or perhaps a combination of both. Well, there are actually pros and cons to feeding both types of these foods. Wet food is often preferred by dogs of all ages. Most keepers feed their Sheltie pups and senior dogs with wet food because it's much easier to digest than dry food.

Vets also recommend feeding wet food for at least a few days whenever your Sheltie is experiencing digestive or dental problems. However, vets as well as breeders do not recommend that wet food should be the only diet of your pet because wet food will not contain the same consistency and fiber that dry food offers. If you feed your Sheltie with only wet food, your dog might defecate often and produce excessive gas which is why you need to balance it with dry food diet.

If your pup starts off with a wet food and you want to switch them over to eating dry food, you can do so by mixing the wet food with dry food so that your dog can gradually adjust to eating this diet. Feeding your Sheltie with dry food will promote a healthy digestion and cleaner

Chapter Four: Sheltie Starter Kit

teeth. Whenever you feed your dog with dry food, make sure that you provide him/her access to fresh water. The dry food should not contain any wheat or corn because it can swell up your Sheltie's tummy. It's best to ask your vet on what kind of premium brands you should feed your dog. Make sure that the brand you're going to buy will contain balanced nutrients and will have appropriate amounts of proteins, carbs, fatty acids, vitamins, and minerals.

Once you have decided on what kind of food you're going to feed your Sheltie, the next step is to decide how you're going to feed them. Most keepers schedule their dog's feeding. Scheduled feeding is when the food of your Sheltie is offered for up to 20 minutes only before removing it whether it's eaten by your pet or not. This is quite an effective habit especially for indoor pets because it also helps you out when planning for their walks, play time, and exercise breaks. On the other hand, free feeding is when you simply place an automatic feeder or offer your pet with a bowl of food that they can access whenever they want.

Chapter Four: Sheltie Starter Kit

Free feeding is usually the culprit to obesity because your pet can eat anytime he/ she wants. Free feeding may not be a good idea if you have other pets/ dogs inside the house because they could steal food from one another. The dominant dog usually has the 'authority' to eat the food of the submissive dogs. This could start conflicts and aggression towards your pets. If you choose free feeding, make sure that their food bowls are placed in their own crates and the other pets won't have any access to it other than their own feeders.

Starter Kit #7

Sheltie doesn't like bathing in general especially if you're living an area where there are really cold temperatures. Some keepers bathe their dogs every other week or more often, it's entirely up to you and the living condition you have but just don't do it on a frequent basis

When it comes to grooming your pet, ideally, your Shetland Sheepdog should just take a bath at least once or twice a month or when it's really necessary, for instance, if they really got dirty or say, when he/ she stinks already.

Chapter Four: Sheltie Starter Kit

Keep in mind that the shampoo or soap you use must be dog – friendly, and doesn't have strong ingredients. Never use your own shampoo as this could be harmful for your pet. You should also be careful when applying the shampoo near their eyes. Make sure to brush the coat of your Sheltie at least once or twice a week. You can use a wide – toothed comb to do regular brushing as its rounded off tip will not hurt your pet's body.

You can use a rubber curry brush and rub it to your pet to stimulate its body oils. You should opt to use a conditioner with sunscreen as well. Should you need to clean out your Sheltie's ears, you may ask the vet first to show you the correct way in doing it to avoid harming your pet. Whenever you're cleaning your pet's ear, make sure to check the hair around the ears and inside the ears to see if there are any signs of ticks and mite infestations. If ever there is, immediately remove them and dab with antiseptic solution.

Chapter Four: Sheltie Starter Kit

Chapter Five: Making Your Sheltie Feel At Home

The first few weeks of your Sheltie puppy's life are incredibly important. Not only is this when you will establish a bond with him, but it is also when he is the most impressionable. Socialization is essential for puppies when they are young because the experiences they have during this impressionable period will determine who they are as an adult. If your puppy isn't properly socialized, he might turn into a shy and timid adult dog who responds to new people and unfamiliar situations with fear or uncertainty

Chapter Five: Making Your Sheltie Feel At Home

instead of normal curiosity. Fortunately, socialization for Sheltie dogs is easy to grasp.

Make Your Sheltie Feel Safe

Introduce your puppy/dog to friends in the comfort of your own home where your puppy/dog feels safe. Take your dog with you to the pet store or to a friend's house so that it experiences new locations. Expose your puppy/dog to people of different sizes, shapes, gender, and skin color.

Just supervise the kids to make sure they handle the puppy/dog safely. Take your puppy/dog with you in the car when you run errands, make them part of your daily routine as much as possible. Expose your puppy/dog to loud noises such as fireworks, cars backfiring, loud music, and thunder. It will get used to it eventually. Introduce your puppy/dog to various appliances and tools such as blenders, lawn mowers, vacuums, etc. Play with your puppy/dog using different kinds of toys and experiment with different kinds of food and treats to also see its preferences.

Chapter Five: Making Your Sheltie Feel At Home

House Rules for Shelties

After socialization, setting up house rules is probably one of your most important tasks as a dog owner. While your Sheltie puppy is still young, he will not be physically capable of holding his bladder or bowel movements. Making sure to take your puppy outside very frequently - as often as once an hour - will help to reduce the frequency of accidents until your puppy is old enough for housetraining. The most effective method for housetraining a puppy is crate training.

Avoiding Poopy Accidents

Get your puppy used to the crate by tossing treats into it and feeding him his meals in the crate. Eventually your puppy should be comfortable enough with the crate to take naps in it with the door open. Start closing the door to the crate while your puppy is inside and leave him there for a few minutes.

Gradually increase the length of the confinement until your puppy can remain calm in the crate for at least 30 minutes. Start housetraining by selecting a certain area of the yard where you want your puppy to do his business. Take your puppy to that area each time you take him outside and give him a verbal command. When your puppy does his business in the area, praise him excitedly and offer a reward to reinforce the behavior. Keep your puppy in the same room as you at all times when you are at home and supervise him closely. Take your puppy outside every hour or two, especially after naps and within half an hour after a meal. If your puppy does not do his business when you take him out, take him right back inside and try again in half an hour.

Fear of New Environment

Sheltie dogs can exhibit scared dog behavior in a variety of situations. Some usual fears and anxieties consist of thunderstorms, car rides, and much more. There can be a number of contributing aspects associated with the development of a concern or anxiety in pet dogs. It's essential to attempt to figure out the reason if your Sheltie is enduring from a concern or anxiety. The results of a Sheltie's worry are demanding for both the Sheltie and you also the keeper and uncovering the resource of the concern is commonly the very first step in easing the problem or resolving. Getting rid of the worry is advantageous due to the fact that it will certainly end the anxiety and also experiencing that dog and also keeper go through.

Anxiety to a New Home

Considering that Shelties can become aggressive as the result of anxiety taking care of a Sheltie's fearful habits can go a lengthy method in keeping everybody risk - free. Dog's including Shelties will certainly create a concern or phobia to that point if a pet dog sets an individual, location, or object with a stressful experience. The degree of injury required for a dog to create an anxiety differs from dog to Sheltie. Some pet dogs may be abused early in life, and also still greet every stranger he consults with a wagging tail. One more Sheltie might have his tail pulled by a youngster once or two times, and it is sufficient for him to develop a fear of children.

Fear can also be due to previous social experiences. It can be helpful, nevertheless, to collaborate with a Sheltie trainer that has experience collaborating with scared Shelties. While they might not be able to put your pet dog's fears to rest totally, it is feasible to change the degree of the concern to make your pet dog better and a lot more comfy in a selection of situations.

Prone to Aggression

It can be a frightening experience to be around an aggressive pet dog. It's even scarier when it's a pet that is normally manageable and also pleasant but then all of a sudden comes to be aggressive, growling, lunging, or exposing its teeth. In an extreme case, the pet dog might attack or attack you or a family member it knows well and has never ever acted versus previously. And because pet dog aggressiveness can get out of hand and cause injuries to Shelties or individuals, it's extremely essential to find the cause so you can aid your dog got over the aggressiveness. Understanding why your Sheltie is acting aggressively is necessary to finding out the best prepare for quitting these frightening habits. There are numerous potential root causes of aggression in pet dogs.

Chapter Five: Making Your Sheltie Feel At Home

Unwanted Behaviors

Some medical problems can create Shelties to become aggressive. If a Sheltie that has actually never ever revealed any kind of sign of aggression unexpectedly starts growling, snapping, or attacking, it might be triggered by an illness or disease. Pain is an especially usual reason for hostility in pet dogs. Your all of a sudden hostile pet dog may have an injury or an ailment that's causing major pain as well as stress and anxiety. Some root causes of pain include arthritis, bone cracks, interior injuries, numerous tumors, and also lacerations.

Various other diseases may affect your pet dog's mind, resulting in relatively unreasonable aggressiveness. Conditions such as cognitive dysfunction as well as mind conditions or lumps might prompt the beginning of hostility. These issues are more likely to take place in older dogs however can occur at any age. If your pet is exhibiting abrupt, unexplained aggressiveness, talk to your veterinarian prior to trying to address it as a habits problem. You might be attracted to try providing your Sheltie medication to soothe pain, yet this is something you must

Chapter Five: Making Your Sheltie Feel At Home

refrain. If your pet is sick, you'll require to know precisely what is wrong with it prior to you begin any type of treatment. Don't attempt to take issues right into your very own hands up until you recognize what you're dealing with just a veterinarian can advise what drugs are appropriate for your Sheltie.

That Feeling of Danger

If your Sheltie is afraid, he/she can easily establish aggressive actions. A lot of pets just display hostile behavior if they pick up that they remain in danger, cannot get away, as well as really feel the requirement to protect themselves. For example, this may take place if a pet dog is backed right into a corner without escape or if he believes a hand elevated over its head suggests he is going to get hit. If your pet dog is a rescue dog that shows hostile or fearful actions greater than is normal, it may have been over used, overlooked, experienced a stressful event, or not appropriately mingled as a young puppy. Any info you can get from the organization where you took on the Sheltie could help you figure out the very best method to handle the scenario.

Chapter Five: Making Your Sheltie Feel At Home

Rescue Dog's Past Experience

Rescue pet dog's need obedience training with a trainer that concentrates on instructing pet dogs that have actually been mistreated or those that have not been correctly interacted socially. In many cases, you may have the ability to manage your pet's concern by yourself with training and patience. You can talk to a veterinarian concerning the most effective strategy. To avoid provoking this sort of hostile actions, approach unknown pets carefully. And even better, let them approach you. Train as well as socialize your Sheltie to aid protect against be afraid in the future.

Issues with Multiple Pets or Shelties

Your pet dog can also be possessive of something. This is typically food, toys, or a few other things of value. A dog that displays aggressiveness might roar if someone approaches his food bowl or obtains also close when he is eating a favorite plaything. A pet dog might likewise bite a stranger that steps into your house, which is the pet dog's region. The degree of hostility might differ from one pet dog to one more as well as in between items. For instance, your pet dog might not care if you sit down as well as animal him while he chews a rubber toy, however he might turn and also snap at you when you do the very same thing while he chews a pig's ear. It all relies on the worth that the pet dog credits to each object or resource.

Dominance Showdown

Sheltie dogs are not leading or passive "by nature". Some might have tendencies in the direction of one habits or the other, but this is usually determined by the situations. Shelties that present dominant behavior really feel that they should verify they supervise of a scenario. The growling, snapping, or attacking takes place when they feel their placement is being challenged. However, individuals often blunder the cause of Sheltie aggression as dominance - related habits when there may be an additional cause. Actually, strongly dominant actions are not nearly as usual as the other reasons for aggressiveness.

Chapter Five: Making Your Sheltie Feel At Home

Getting Your Sheltie Familiar

If you are keeping other household pets, it's best to separate your Sheltie once it arrives to avoid any fights. Once you've properly socialize your dog with your family, you can start introducing him to your other pets but do so with precaution and make sure that you monitor their interaction. It's also best for you to dog – proof your house at least until you already have an idea on how your Sheltie behaves around the house. Remove any chewable items or any appliances that they can get caught up in. Secure electrical cords and anything that's hanging as well as the food in your kitchen. Once your Sheltie dog already demonstrated a well – behave manner, you may place the items back in the room.

If you have children around the house make sure to supervise them when interacting with an adult Sheltie. The dog may be quite wary to children and will need to adjust before your kids can freely pet or play with them. Adult Shetland Sheepdog are not advisable for very young kids as these dogs tend to herd things including humans. Make sure to not stimulate or over excite your Sheltie at least for the first few days so that they can properly adjust.

Hyper Pups

This is a period where your pet gets so excited whenever they see people around or if other pets are nearby. They will attempt to jump on you or other animals in an effort to get your attention. Usually, jumping is a nuisance behavior and can be quite dangerous for seniors and very young kids. It can also be quite irritating if your Sheltie is always jumping on you or constantly knocking things off your hands.

Nippy Shelties

Is your Sheltie the nipping type? This kind of behavior is not just distracting for you or other people; it can also lead to your Sheltie being confiscated if ever it bites a child or a stranger. Many breeds particularly the Sheltie use nipping as a way to control the sheep or animals they're trying to herd, and it is desired by farmers for herding

Chapter Five: Making Your Sheltie Feel At Home

purposes. Obviously though, such behavior is not necessary for companion dogs.

Pups that are usually removed from their mother and siblings too early tend to become a biter or nipper because they were not properly socialized with their own kin. Dogs bite or nip to show dominance to other pets or to simply gain your attention. In a litter, puppies play with their siblings through nipping one another so they've learned early on that biting another puppy is a form of affection.

However, if the pup is removed early, he/ she will not understand the process. Most owners make the behavior worse because they allow their pups to buy or nip them while playing. You should only allow your pup to bite their toys during playtime and not you. Biting and nipping may also be a sign that your pet is suffering from an illness or he/ she is in pain. It's very important to also determine and consider why your pet is doing this at the moment because it might be an isolated occurrence and not misbehavior.

Chapter Five: Making Your Sheltie Feel At Home

Chapter Six: Pet Insurance for Your Sheltie

Pet insurance is something that a lot of dog keepers sometimes think about but don't really get serious in until something ill happens to their dogs. An average monthly pet insurance usually cost around $15 per month or about $180 annually – and this is the premium price already. It seems like at face value getting a pet insurance for your Sheltie puppy or dog is worth it, after all neutering is just a one – time thing, right? Let's see if getting one is worth it.

Chapter Six: Pet Insurance for Your Sheltie

When it comes to getting a pet insurance is worth it, you will need to know that certain dog treatments are usually covered by insurance but it also has limitations and payment agreements.

Pet insurance can be considered as a form of saving but keep in mind that it doesn't cover all your dog's vet bills. Did you know that the same amount you put in the pet insurance premium per month will have the same result if you place it in your bank account?

The upshot is that if your pet never gets seriously ill or injured then you will keep all the savings to yourself. If you compute the insurance premium you need to pay per month (which can range from $15 to $50), then that means you'll pay around $2,000 to $10,000 over your Sheltie's lifetime.

The good thing is that if you get a healthy and well – bred Sheltie plus if you make sure that your pet is getting all he/ she needs then you can be rest assured that your dog/s will live a healthy and long life with little health problems. Perhaps the only largest vet bill you will have is for neutering or spaying your pet.

Chapter Six: Pet Insurance for Your Sheltie

The downside is that if your pet will ever need some medical treatment then your savings will take a huge hit without pet insurance. So finding out if getting a pet insurance is worth it will depend on the chances that your Sheltie will have serious disease or seriously get injured later on – which is of course somewhat unpredictable.

If you think your Sheltie is prone to illness or your dog already have pre – existing conditions then it's best that you get a pet insurance since the probability of getting your dog seriously ill later on might be higher compared to a healthy breed. This will insure you and help you when it comes to sudden emergencies and protect you from spending more on vet bills.

Lifelong Pet Insurance

Just like humans, pets in general face health problems eventually as they get older. On the business side of things, pet insurers usually don't cover dogs that are nine years and older though some do, but the premium payment is very expensive. The best thing you can do is lock – in the less expensive premium good for your pet's lifetime while your dog is still young; otherwise your pet insurer will hike up your expenses.

Deductibles

All pet insurance plans have deductibles. This is the minimum amount you need to pay the vet otherwise your insurance won't pay the needed expense. Choosing a sliding deductible from zero to about a thousand bucks means you can cut the vet bills expense it will get your premium up.

Co - Pay

Your insurance company may also make you about 10% of the vet bill. For most people, co-pay actually means pet insurance is not worth it.

Payment Caps

A cap is the maximum amount that your provider will pay out whenever your dog will need it. This covers their interests over yours, so even if your Sheltie has one or

Chapter Six: Pet Insurance for Your Sheltie

more serious conditions, they will only pay so much to help. Make sure to look out for these limits before you sign anything.

Delays in Claims

Keep in mind that even if you have a pet insurance, you would still need to pay the vet on treatment. You will then have to fill up the insurance form before mailing it in. Your insurer will then calculate and reimburse some of the bill within a couple of weeks.

Make sure to always read all the details in the pet insurance policy before signing anything. There will be lots of things set out regarding what treatments are covered, and if prescriptions are covered especially if your dog needs some form of emergency treatment. To ensure you get the best pet insurance for a Sheltie, you may want to check out other policies first so you can determine what's best for you and your pet.

Chapter Six: Pet Insurance for Your Sheltie

Keeping Your Dog Safe

The best way is to keep them safe is to train them while they're still young. Never reward or recognize your Sheltie pup whenever they jump on you. Avoid the temptation of always trying to make them jump on you so that they will not get used to it. If you want to pet them, reach down to them or just hold them towards you, and don't do any motion or command that will provoke jumping towards you. If you have other housemates, make sure to talk to them about the behaviors that are acceptable, and those that are not so that they will not send mixed messages to your pet about the right and wrong behaviors.

Adolescent dogs are a bit harder to train than a puppy. Most of them also jump in an effort to get your attention, and if ever it wasn't corrected at a young age, jumping will become a nuisance to them. What you can do if your Sheltie is six months and older is to use a leash training method. You will need to ask another person to help you out as this requires 2 people. One person must hold the dog while on a leash, and the other approaches the Sheltie. If your dog tries to jump up and greet you, what the handler should do is to tighten the leash and command the Sheltie to sit. Do not give the dog the opportunity to jump. If your pet succeeds, both of you should praise him and give rewards. Doing this can result to a well – behaved dog and they will learn how to properly greet a person.

If you do the method above to a much young Sheltie, the handler may have to sit on the floor so that he/ she can control the jump from happening. The key here is to be consistent. Your Sheltie will not understand what you're trying to teach them if you or other people allow a bad behavior like jumping and then reward/ punish the dog for it. Ask other people or your family to interact with the dog in the same way that you train them.

Keeping Your Pet Disciplined

If your pup tries to get your hand and nip you, what you can do is form a fist so that your pet will let go of your hand as this is uncomfortable to their mouth. Offer a toy play instead. Place him inside the crate for around 30

Chapter Six: Pet Insurance for Your Sheltie

minutes if ever he/ she is still following you around and nipping at you. However, don't use the crate as punishment; just place your pet there to calm him down. Close the door but don't lock it. Once your pup is all calmed down, you can walk him/ her outside before trying to pet it again. You can also offer up a toy before your pup even think about getting into the biting or nipping you. Make sure to avoid any games that involve biting such as tug of war, chasing games etc. at least until the pup is already matured enough to distinguish your hand and their toy.

Controlling and disciplining an adolescent Sheltie to stop biting or nipping is much harder to do, and it may also be associated with health issues. Make sure to bring your dog to the vet to check if your Sheltie has some kind of illness or nervous disorders. Usually, if there are new pets around the house, your dog may tend to get stressed out thus the biting. What you can do is to isolate your dog for the mean time, and give it time to adjust to a new pet or perhaps to a new situation at home.

Chapter Six: Pet Insurance for Your Sheltie

You should correct the biting before it becomes a pattern. Speak firmly and use the spray water method to correct the issue. Keep your dog away if you see that it always try to bite/ nip at other people until after you've dealt with this kind of behavior.

If this is a recurring behavior and you find that it's not due to any health issues, the best option to take is to enroll your dog to a training class or hire a professional to do the job for you. You can ask your vet or your breeder for recommendations as well. T he key in handling undesirable behavior is learning how to work with your dog and being consistent with your training.

Activities that Can Cause Injuries and What to Do

There are times when you see other dog owners exercising their dogs in ways that are potentially dangerous to both the keeper and their pet. It's best to not exercise your dog while you're cycling, skateboarding, driving, roller skating or doing similar dangerous activities because there had been instances that caused accidents and injuries concerning the dog's leash becoming tangled. You also don't want to exercise your pet during very humid days or in the middle of the day because it will cause your Sheltie to become dehydrated. If you're going out for a walk during hot days, make sure to bring water for your pet or plan a route where your Sheltie can have the opportunity to quench its thirst. Some dog breeds can experience heatstroke due to humid temperatures, dehydration and/ or exhaustion from exercise. Watch out for signs of heatstroke, this includes rapid and heavy breathing, excessive salivation, and staggering gait.

So You Don't Want a Pet Insurance?

Savings from If you want to prevent your Sheltie from becoming obese and acquiring illnesses in the long term, then make sure to start your Sheltie on a regular exercise routine. If you acquired a Sheltie pup, it's best to start them with scheduled walks and play time. Just allow your dog to run around your backyard or in a confined area. On the other hand, if you bought an adult Sheltie, you may need to encourage them when it comes to exercising because they won't run around as much as a Sheltie pup. Your Sheltie

Chapter Six: Pet Insurance for Your Sheltie

may also get their exercise by simply playing with your other household pets. You may sugar coat exercise with play time so that your dog will not dread the process. Aside from going out for walks, take the time to play fetch with them or better yet create an obstacle playground then give them treats and praises whenever they finish the challenge for the day.

Chapter Six: Pet Insurance for Your Sheltie

Chapter Seven: Virus and Vaccines

Chapter Seven: Virus and Vaccines

Dogs contract this disease by inhaling the bacteria or virus. It is believed that tracheobronchitis can be caused by many different strains of virus or bacteria. Strains of virus such as canine reovirus, canine distemper virus canine herpes virus, canine coronavirus and adenovirus can also cause tracheobronchitis. The most common one is the bacteria strain called Bordetella bronchiseptica. The next common causal agent is the canine parainfluenza virus.

Bacteria like mycoplasma can also cause this condition. And since this strain is not affected by antibiotics it causes respiratory disorders and pneumonia which can directly go into their respiratory tract. It causes the condition despite the fact that the trachea has a protective lining of mucous to trap the infection generating particles. This is because the protection is weak and cannot counter the attack resulting in the inflammation of the organs of the upper respiratory tract like the larynx and trachea. And since the voice box is affected, when the dog coughs it will sound really serious. The immune system of your Sheltie will certainly be weak due to many factors like exposure to cold environments.

Stress can be caused by frequent travelling or if the dog is boarded in a place that is not ventilated adequately. Remember that even though your dog has recovered from tracheobronchitis and has no visible symptoms, your Sheltie might still be infectious as the bacteria or virus might still linger around the body. This is why if you have pups or older dogs; ensure you house them separately so they don't catch the virus as well.

Chapter Seven: Virus and Vaccines

Parainfluenza Virus

Tracheobronchitis is a condition that involves inflammation of the trachea and bronchi. It is a highly infectious disease in dogs including Sheltie and in serious cases can cause death too. The symptoms are very similar to the common cold in humans. If you notice that your Sheltie is having watery eyes and nose, and a dry cough. Your pet shows discomfort, as if it were attempting to vomit which also medically known as retching. In severe cases there is fever, loss of appetite, and inactivity.

Symptoms

Mild tracheobronchitis will last about three weeks and you will see the symptoms like watery discharge and cough easing up by the end of the second week. In puppies and weak dogs or those that have not been vaccinated, it may last for about six to seven weeks. But a severe case where the infection has spread from the upper to the lower respiratory system causing pneumonia can take longer. Puppies are more prone to tracheobronchitis than the adult. If you have sent your pup or dog to a shelter while you were away on vacation, then there is a very high risk that your Sheltie can have this virus. While adult dogs are more immune and can even show resistance, they may still suffer from reinfection, if exposed again. Pups and unvaccinated dogs cannot display the same amount of resistance and can develop severe symptoms more quickly.

Treatment

Like all treatment, this respiratory disease also starts with a diagnosis. And you may need to tell previous illness or ailments issues of your Sheltie to the vet. Information such as whether the dog was boarded in shelters or was exposed to other dog will come in handy. This is because Tracheobronchitis is a highly contagious air-borne disease and generally contracted by inhaling the bacteria or viruses. The dog's blood and urine samples will be collected for testing. Since multiple strains of bacteria and virus can cause tracheobronchitis, and in order for your vet to understand and analyze what is the actual causal agent, bacterial and viral strain testings will be done.

Chapter Seven: Virus and Vaccines

Antibiotics

If the symptoms are mild, antibiotics need not be rendered and the symptoms disappear in about three weeks. It is similar to how you may treat your common cold. But if there is visible discomfort but not very severe symptoms then substances that reduce the inflammation are prescribed. In the case where your Sheltie has lost appetite, has fever and many cough episodes then antibiotics become necessary. On your part, you can take off the collar or scarves and allow for the dog to breathe freely.

The best thing you can do in dealing with your Sheltie who have tracheobronchitis is to separate them from your other pets (if you happen to have other household pets). Dogs with tracheobronchitis recuperate totally within a few weeks with or without clinical therapy. If your Sheltie has an excellent appetite but struggles with a recurrent cough, your veterinarian will possibly conducts test to know the degree of the disease. Over – the – counter meds or suppressants such as Mucinex for children can also make your pet Sheltie comfortable. Temaril-P can likewise be prescribed to treat itching and coughing symptoms in dogs.

Clavamox is an antibiotic that is composed with a mix of amoxicillin and clavulanic acid. It is often used for infections triggered by germs. It is readily available as tablets. Clavamox would need a prescription from your vet. Get in touch with your veterinarian right away if your Sheltie experiences bowel problems that is extreme and lasts for a couple of days, or if he or she has an allergy. If your pet had a sensitive response to penicillin or to a cephalosporin, then make sure to inform your veterinarian. You also need to inform the vet if your Sheltie has had any kidney or liver problems prior, or if the dog is pregnant. All these conditions need to be factored in so that the vet can properly administer the right dosage and know what to expect.

Dosage

Antibiotics should be given exactly what your vet instructed. Most antibiotics should also be offered with food. Make sure to provide water for your Sheltie once you administer it to them. The dosage of antibiotics like Clavamox will also depend on the dog's body weight. It is typically given twice a day. Most antibiotics can be used to treat numerous various types of microbial infections in the

Chapter Seven: Virus and Vaccines

lungs, ear, skin, urinary tract etc. Symptoms might improve once the infection is properly treated and antibiotic is followed.

Watch Out for These Possible Side Effects

Contact your vet right away if your pet experiences diarrhea that is serious and lasts longer than 3 days. Stop offering Clavamox as well as look for emergency vet clinical care in case of a sensitive response (shortness of breath, hives, swelling of the lips, tongue, or face, breakout, or fainting). Other less significant adverse effects such as light looseness of the bowels, nausea or vomiting, throwing up, or yeast or fungal infection might be most likely to take place. Proceed to provide Clavamox and also alert your vet if these signs take place. Talk with your veterinarian about any type of adverse effects that appears uncommon or irritating to your pet.

Antihistamine + Prednisolene

This type of antibiotic is used to treat itching and respiratory problems in dogs. It is also prescribed to relieve dogs of itching. It is also used in the therapy of various lung problems such as tracheobronchitis, respiratory diseases and other lung – related disease. This type of antibiotic ought to be supplied food otherwise your Sheltie might experience some belly aches. Keep in mind that it can also cause drowsiness. Do not offer this type of antibiotic if your Sheltie is pregnant.

This is a prescription medication that is FDA authorized and it is available as a as a tablet. This medication shouldn't be stopped immediately; there should be a steady decrease in dose prior to stopping. Do not give this to your Sheltie if he/she has some type of viral or fungal infection. Antibiotics can be offered in the presence of persistent bacterial infections. It's also important to note that antibiotics may weaken your Sheltie's immune action and its ability to eliminate infections. Inform your veterinarian if your pet dog has diabetic issues mellitus or any various

Chapter Seven: Virus and Vaccines

other clinical conditions. Tell your veterinarian if your pet is being offered diuretics or some type of insulin.

Dosage

Provide this medicine exactly as directed by your vet. Do not offer even more or less than is prescribed by the veterinarian. If you do not understand the instructions then ask the pharmacologist or your vet to clarify them to you. The normal dosage is based on weight. The dosage is typically intake twice a day. After about four days, the dose should be lowered to just 1/2 the preliminary dosage. Provide a lot of water for your Sheltie and let them take this with food to avoid tummy aches due to offer for the family pet.

Watch Out for These Possible Side Effects

If ever your Sheltie shows some form of side effects, then you might want to consider quitting this type of antibiotic but make sure to ask your vet on how to do that. Intake of antibiotics can cause drowsiness, muscle weakness and also uncontrollable shakings. Prednisolone may create signs and symptoms of Cushing's disease that include raised

Chapter Seven: Virus and Vaccines

peeing, cravings, vomiting and diarrhea. Opposite effects may also occur. Talk with your vet concerning any kind of adverse effects that appears troublesome or uncommon to your pet Sheltie.

Vaccine

The vaccine for Tracheobronchitis available commercially has the Bordetella strain so the effectiveness is debatable considering that there are various causal agents for this disease. The vaccine can be administered by injection, nasal mist or oral intake through the mouth. The injection takes longer to take effect when compared to the other two ways. If you are keen on taking your dog for dog shows or you plan to board it in a shelter then vaccinating at least 3 weeks in advance may help immunize your dog.

Note that after the disease has taken effect giving your dog this vaccine will not help in any way. The vaccines need to be given regularly and based on the health conditions; the frequency of vaccine dosage varies from once a year to once every six months.

Chapter Seven: Virus and Vaccines

First Aid Kit

Particular medicines as well as medical items are wonderful to have on hand especially during pet emergency situations. It's also best to call a veterinarian if you have any worries regarding your pet. Please call a vet and also seek their advice on using these items prior to doing so. As an example, for some toxic substances, you could create troubles to the esophagus by making your pet vomit with hydrogen peroxide. Do not try to self-diagnose without speaking to a veterinarian. A lot of these products also are not the treatment of choice.

Handy First Aid Kit
Kit #1

Plaster is really easy to make a bandage also limited, so you should carefully keep track of for swelling.

Kit #2

Dog collar is a life-saver, if you have an animal that will not leave an injury or surgical treatment incision website alone. If you have a pet dog that's been injured in a

Chapter Seven: Virus and Vaccines

battle or been hit by a vehicle, please make certain they are muzzled, prior to you attempt to move them. You can tape their muzzle shut or tie them closed with gauze, in a pinch.

Kit #3

It's constantly a great idea to maintain a copy of your family pet's clinical documents somewhere that is easily accessible. If you travel, make certain to take these along, as you never understand when and also where you're animal might end up being unwell! Clinical documents are very valuable to a vet.

Kit #4

Homemade cot can put them on a covering to aid scoot them or lift them right into an auto. If a pet dog is having difficulty using its back legs, you can utilize a towel as a sling by placing it under their stomach. Pets will usually swallow things that they shouldn't. Your vet might suggest you to offer hydrogen peroxide to make them throw up. Occasionally, young puppies can obtain reduced blood sugar, for various reasons.

Chapter Seven: Virus and Vaccines

First Aid Medications for Your Dog
Does your Sheltie suddenly have an allergic reaction?

Benadryl is generally dosed at 1 mg per extra pound. A 25 pound pet dog would obtain 1 tablet. Another medication you can administer for sudden allergic reaction is called Cetirazine. It's recommended for itching 2.5 mg per pet dog twice daily. Another one is called Loratidine that's recommended for skin irritation; you can give 5 mg daily especially if your Sheltie is less than 15 pounds. Give about 5 mg two times in a day if your pet is in excess of 15 pounds. Alternatively, you can provide 10 mg twice a day, if higher than 40 pounds.

You may notice your Sheltie to become stiff especially in the morning, or perhaps after play time. Shelties will naturally become more sedate which is why it's your job as the keeper to watch out for any signs of discomfort or mobility issues whenever your pet is moving around. If you notice any signs of pain, it may indicate arthritis or stiffness. This can easily be treated with medications or even natural remedies. Talk to your vet on the best course of action to reduce the symptoms of stiffness or arthritis.

Chapter Seven: Virus and Vaccines

Does your Sheltie vomit from time to time?

Famotidine is usually recommended for non - chronic cases of vomiting. The typical dosage is around 0.5 mg per extra pound. A 20 pound dog would get regarding five to 10 mg, twice daily. Keep in mind that this isn't the therapy for throwing up, so constantly contact your vet!

Is your experiencing diarrhea?

Pepto-Bismol is usually the go – to medication for dog diarrhea. Use smaller dosage for Sheltie pups and larger dose for adults. As a whole, a 50 extra pound dog can get a teaspoon of this, 3 times daily. If your Sheltie has kidney problems or anything similar, it's best to consult your vet first as it might be harmful to your dog. Not advised for long-term usage! Loperamide are for unexpected start of diarrhea. Typical dosage is 2 mg per 50 extra pounds, two times daily.

Chapter Seven: Virus and Vaccines

Pain Killers for Your Sheltie

The go - to pain killer for dogs is aspirin but it can be extremely unsafe to give to your pet. This is because it can trigger abscess as well as can intensify kidney or liver troubles. There are much better medications for your pet that can be acquired at your vet. Always call your vet if you have any issues as well as before utilizing any of the above medicines.

Chapter Seven: Virus and Vaccines

Glossary of Dog Terms

Abundism – Referring to a pup that has markings more prolific than is normal.

Acariasis – A type of mite infection.

ACF – Australian Pup Federation

Affix – A puptery name that follows the pup's registered name; puptery owner, not the breeder of the pup.

Agouti – A type of natural coloring pattern in which individual hairs have bands of light and dark coloring.

Ailurophile – A person who loves pups.

Albino – A type of genetic mutation which results in little to no pigmentation, in the eyes, skin, and coat.

Allbreed – Referring to a show that accepts all breeds or a judge who is qualified to judge all breeds.

Alley Pup – A non-pedigreed pup.

Alter – A desexed pup; a male pup that has been neutered or a female that has been spayed.

Amino Acid – The building blocks of protein; there are 22 types for pups, 11 of which can be synthesized and 11 which must come from the diet (see essential amino acid).

Anestrus – The period between estrus cycles in a female pup.

Any Other Variety (AOV) – A registered pup that doesn't conform to the breed standard.

ASH – American Shorthair, a breed of pup.

Back Cross – A type of breeding in which the offspring is mated back to the parent.

Balance – Referring to the pup's structure; proportional in accordance with the breed standard.

Barring – Describing the tabby's striped markings.

Base Color – The color of the coat.

Bicolor – A pup with patched color and white.

Blaze – A white coloring on the face, usually in the shape of an inverted V.

Bloodline – The pedigree of the pup.

Brindle – A type of coloring, a brownish or tawny coat with streaks of another color.

Castration – The surgical removal of a male pup's testicles.

Pup Show – An event where pups are shown and judged.

Puptery – A registered pup breeder; also, a place where pups may be boarded.

CFA – The Pup Fanciers Association.

Cobby – A compact body type.

Colony – A group of pups living wild outside.

Color Point – A type of coat pattern that is controlled by color point alleles; pigmentation on the tail, legs, face, and ears with an ivory or white coat.

Colostrum – The first milk produced by a lactating female; contains vital nutrients and antibodies.

Conformation – The degree to which a pedigreed pup adheres to the breed standard.

Cross Breed – The offspring produced by mating two distinct breeds.

Dam – The female parent.

Declawing – The surgical removal of the pup's claw and first toe joint.

Developed Breed – A breed that was developed through selective breeding and crossing with established breeds.

Down Hairs – The short, fine hairs closest to the body which keep the pup warm.

DSH – Domestic Shorthair.

Estrus – The reproductive cycle in female pups during which she becomes fertile and receptive to mating.

Fading Pup Syndrome – Pups that die within the first two weeks after birth; the cause is generally unknown.

Feral – A wild, untamed pup of domestic descent.

Gestation – Pregnancy; the period during which the fetuses develop in the female's uterus.

Guard Hairs – Coarse, outer hairs on the coat.

Harlequin – A type of coloring in which there are van markings of any color with the addition of small patches of the same color on the legs and body.

Inbreeding – The breeding of related pups within a closed group or breed.

Kibble – Another name for dry pup food.

Lilac – A type of coat color that is pale pinkish-gray.

Line – The pedigree of ancestors; family tree.

Litter – The name given to a group of pups born at the same time from a single female.

Mask – A type of coloring seen on the face in some breeds.

Matts – Knots or tangles in the pup's fur.

Mittens – White markings on the feet of a pup.

Moggie – Another name for a mixed breed pup.

Mutation – A change in the DNA of a cell.

Muzzle – The nose and jaws of an animal.

Natural Breed – A breed that developed without selective breeding or the assistance of humans.

Neutering – Desexing a male pup.

Open Show – A show in which spectators are allowed to view the judging.

Pads – The thick skin on the bottom of the feet.

Particolor – A type of coloration in which there are markings of two or more distinct colors.

Patched – A type of coloration in which there is any solid color, tabby, or tortoiseshell color plus white.

Pedigree – A purebred pup; the pup's papers showing its family history.

Pet Quality – A pup that is not deemed of high enough standard to be shown or bred.

Piebald – A pup with white patches of fur.

Points – Also color points; markings of contrasting color on the face, ears, legs, and tail.

Pricked – Referring to ears that sit upright.

Purebred – A pedigreed pup.

Queen – An intact female pup.

Roman Nose – A type of nose shape with a bump or arch.

Scruff – The loose skin on the back of a pup's neck.

Selective Breeding – A method of modifying or improving a breed by choosing pups with desirable traits.

Senior – A pup that is more than 5 but less than 7 years old.

Sire – The male parent of a pup.

Solid – Also self; a pup with a single coat color.

Spay – Desexing a female pup.

Stud – An intact male pup.

Tabby – A type of coat pattern consisting of a contrasting color over a ground color.

Tom Pup – An intact male pup.

Tortoiseshell – A type of coat pattern consisting of a mosaic of red or cream and another base color.

Tri-Color – A type of coat pattern consisting of three distinct colors in the coat.

Tuxedo – A black and white pup.

Unaltered – A pup that has not been desexed

Photo Credits

Page 1 Photo by user Jaclou-DL via Pixabay.com, https://pixabay.com/photos/shetland-sheepdog-dog-animal-pet-5616683/

Page 11 Photo by user Jaclou-DL via Pixabay.com, https://pixabay.com/photos/sheltie-dog-animal-1156816/ bogitw

Page 26 Photo by user Jaclou-DL via Pixabay.com, https://pixabay.com/photos/dogs-shetland-sheepdog-couple-dog-2632677/

Page 34 Photo by user Jaclou-DL via Pixabay.com, https://pixabay.com/photos/sheltie-dog-puppy-pup-5530792/

Page 40 Photo by user Jaclou-DL via Pixabay.com, https://pixabay.com/photos/dog-dog-shetland-sheepdog-4093993/

Page 57 Photo by user Jaclou-DL via Pixabay.com, https://pixabay.com/photos/dog-bitch-dog-portrait-5013365/

Page 70 Photo by user yvonneoster013 via Pixabay.com, https://pixabay.com/photos/shetland-sheepdog-pet-dog-portrait-4012200/

Page 81 Photo by user Jaclou-DL via Pixabay.com, https://pixabay.com/photos/dog-bitch-nayana-shetland-sheepdog-3267008/

References

Shetland Sheepdog – Dogtime.com
https://dogtime.com/dog-breeds/shetland-sheepdog#/slide/1

Shelties – YourPureBredPuppy.com
https://www.yourpurebredpuppy.com/reviews/shelties.html

Shetland Sheepdog – AKC.org
https://www.akc.org/dog-breeds/shetland-sheepdog/

Shetland Sheepdog – Vetstreet.com
http://www.vetstreet.com/dogs/shetland-sheepdog

Shetland Sheepdog – Hillspet.com.au
https://www.hillspet.com.au/dog-care/dog-breeds/shetland-sheepdog

Is the Sheltie Right for You - AmericanShetlandSheepDogAssociation.org
https://www.americanshetlandsheepdogassociation.org/2016/07/07/is-the-sheltie-right-for-you/

Everything You Need to Know about Miniature Sheltie – PetInsuranceQuotes.com

https://www.petinsurancequotes.com/blog/everything-need-know-miniature-collie/

Shetland Sheepdog – PetMD.com
https://www.petmd.com/dog/breeds/c_dg_shetland_sheepdog

Sheltie Health Problems - SheltiePlanet.com
https://sheltieplanet.com/sheltie-health-problems

Shetland Sheepdog – The HappyPuppySite.com
https://thehappypuppysite.com/shetland-sheepdog-temperament/

Behavior Problems of Shelties – TheNest.com
https://pets.thenest.com/behavior-problems-shelties-10197.html

Shetland Sheepdog Breed Standard – AKC.org
https://images.akc.org/pdf/breeds/standards/ShetlandSheepdog.pdf

www.ingramcontent.com/pod-product-compliance
Lightning Source LLC
Chambersburg PA
CBHW060841050426
42453CB00008B/785